Designed for **Living**
Life as God intended

A step-by-step unfolding of how problems arise in the personality and God's plan for overcoming them.

8 Bible-based sessions for women

Jeannette Barwick and Helena Wilkinson

Designed for **Living**
Life as God intended

8 Bible-based sessions for women

Jeannette Barwick and Helena Wilkinson

Published 2009 by CWR, Waverley Abbey House, Waverley Lane,
Farnham, Surrey GU9 8EP, England. Registered Charity No. 294387.
Registered Limited Company No. 1990308.

For list of National Distributors visit our website www.cwr.org.uk

Unless otherwise indicated, all Scripture references are from the Holy Bible:
New International Version (NIV), copyright © 1973, 1978, 1984 by the
International Bible Society.
NLT: Scripture quotations marked NLT are taken from the *Holy Bible*,
New Living Translation, copyright © 1996, 2004. Used by permission of
Tyndale House Publishers, Inc., Wheaton, Illinois 60189. All rights reserved.
The Message: Scripture taken from *THE MESSAGE.* Copyright © by Eugene
H. Peterson, 1993, 1994, 1995. Used by permission of NavPress Publishing Group.
NKJV: New King James Version copyright © 1982, Thomas Nelson Inc.

* Every reasonable attempt has been made to trace the source of quotations marked *.
Many of the 'Have a Smile' quotations were found on Mary Southerland's website.
** Previously quoted in *My Favourite Stories about Children* by Selwyn Hughes
(Farnham: CWR, 2001).

Concept development, editing, design and production by CWR

Cover image: Getty Images/Digital Vision/Marcy Maloy

Printed in England by Nuffield Press

ISBN: 978-1-85345-523-0

Contents

It's in Christ that we find out who we are
and what we are living for.
Long before we first heard of Christ
and got our hopes up,
he had his eye on us, had designs on us
for glorious living,
part of the overall purpose he is working out
in everything and everyone.

Taken from Ephesians 1 – The Message

Introduction

Jeannette Barwick

One of the most exciting and empowering concepts I have ever come across in over fifty years of the Christian life is the biblical fact that we are made to function according to a divine design. Soon after joining CWR in the 1980s I was exposed to their biblical teaching on how God made us and what makes us tick. My own life has been greatly impacted by understanding the implications of what it means to be made in God's image.

What does it really mean to be made in the image of God? And how does understanding this fact empower us in our spiritual lives? In this workbook we have sought to break open the biblical truth on which these concepts are based and to show how although the original design was marred by sin, through Christ all aspects of that design may be redeemed and restored in each of our lives.

It has been a great joy in my life to take these concepts and present them to hundreds of women at Waverley Abbey House and at our regional seminars. Nothing satisfies me more, as a teacher of biblical truth, than to spend time helping women discover their true identity in Christ. And I have found that nothing empowers a woman more than understanding what it truly means to be made in the image of God and to live in this transforming insight – a way of living life as God intended.

Since Helena and I worked together at Waverley twenty years ago, we have both subsequently had the opportunity to share these principles with many women through our different avenues of ministry. I am thrilled that we now have the opportunity to share these truths with many more through the pages of this workbook.

It is wonderful to see women being released from old patterns of living as they come to understand, often for the first time, how marvellously God has made us and how the Bible shows us that the same characteristics we see in Christ can be seen in our lives also. Whether women are young in the faith or more mature, lives are transformed by these truths. At the end of a seminar in London a woman told me, 'I had always thought, "Well, this is me, I can't change. I'll never be any different." But now I can see that, if I live in harmony with God's design, my way of living can be so different. It's a real revelation and for the first time I've got a sense of hope. I feel like a new person.'

There are many Christians who seem content just to survive, but the intention of God is not that we merely survive but that we thrive. This woman's approach to her situation had enabled her just to survive but with her new understanding came the confident hope that, in and through Christ, she could really thrive.

It is with joy I look to the future, seeking to live my life according to the divine design, knowing that this is where true fulfilment and satisfaction lie. Having turned seventy years of age I am still committed to go on growing in God myself and to seize every opportunity to share these life-transforming truths with others. The deepening understanding that God designed me is the thing that empowers me more than any other as I seek to fulfil His calling on my life. It is my prayer that taking hold of this truth and applying it to your own life will do the same for you.

Making the most of this workbook

Helena Wilkinson

My introduction to the concepts in this workbook was as a student on Waverley's first Institute in Christian Counselling course, back in 1989. The understanding of human nature in the counselling training is that each aspect of our functioning (physical, thinking, choosing, feeling and longing) is so intricately linked to the others that if there is brokenness in one area there tends to be a knock-on effect in the other areas. In addressing the brokenness and the unhealthy ways in which we endeavour to meet our deepest longings, and in coming to God to meet those longings, we are restored into the divine image and so function more effectively in our relationship both with ourselves and with others.

In 1999 Jeannette Barwick skilfully adapted and applied some of the core principles from the course and created a seminar for women, 'Designer Living' (now renamed 'Designed for Living'), focusing on personal growth and maturity. Attending such a seminar can have a profound effect upon our lives and for some the seminar has proved to be a major turning point. However, it is all too easy to be impacted in the moment and then, in the routine or busyness of everyday living, to fail to follow through on things. To help deepen and ingrain the concepts, CWR decided it would be helpful to create a workbook based on the seminar, with the intention of helping to restore women emotionally and spiritually.

The workbook is ideally used as a tool following on from attending a Designed for Living seminar, but it is put together in such a way as to stand alone – should you not be able to attend. It can be used for personal study or for study within a group.

Individual Study

Most of us have a tendency to purchase a workbook with great intentions but, as time goes on, our enthusiasm often dwindles, resulting in an unfinished job. I think it's fair to say that to study a workbook on your own requires discipline and so, to help you to attain your goal of completing it, you will need to bear in mind how much time you can realistically invest each week and what part of the day works best for you. Keeping a journal can be a useful aid for those who want to take the teaching in the workbook a little deeper and find writing a beneficial means to reflect on changes to be made. Perhaps you would also like to consider asking a friend to support you in prayer for the period of your study.

Group Study

Rather than work on your own your preference may be to use the workbook in a group setting, in which case there are two possibilities: a weekend away or weekly group sessions. When using it as a focus for a weekend away, it would be helpful to appoint in advance a group leader and also, perhaps, small group co-ordinators. Whilst the workbook is designed to need very little preparation, thought will be required as to how the sessions are going to be spread across the weekend in order to give sufficient time to the different subjects. It is also invaluable to include a feedback session at the end, allowing time for people to share what has impacted them, as this inevitably brings encouragement.

If you decide to use the workbook for eight weekly sessions, you can apply much of what has already been mentioned, but you have the added luxury of time between the sessions to reflect. You will notice a section headed 'Creative Ideas' which offers ways of including audio and/or visual aids to the session, adding interest and stimulation should you find this helpful. (Preparation time will need to be given to the creative ideas in order to make the most of them.)

Session Format

To enable the smooth running of sessions, each one has been set out in the same format. This also allows the session time to be invested in the content of the workbook. However, planning is still necessary and can usefully involve becoming acquainted with the suggested scriptures and praying for the group sessions in advance.

Besides introductory reading on the subject being addressed, each session includes a number of small sections. 'Explore the Bible' offers biblical references for the subject being covered; 'Ask Yourself' provides the chance to get to know how you honestly think or respond; and 'Take it Deeper' involves addressing issues at a more challenging level. In addition to these there is a little section, 'Have a smile', to allow for a light-hearted moment, and 'Listen to others', a short narrative from someone bringing personal application. Each session includes a short prayer followed by suggested themes should you want to spend additional time praying.

However you find yourself using this workbook the aim is to

help you to understand other people and to unravel your own longings, motives and patterns of thinking and relating. It is Jeannette's and my prayer that, as well as gaining insight and understanding, you will learn to trust God and to validate and care for yourself. This will not only have positive benefits you but for others too, giving them the opportunity to grow in similar ways.

PART 1 –
Considering our design

Life as God intended

The greatest minds are capable of the greatest vices as well as the greatest virtues.

(René Descartes)

Why is it that human beings are capable of doing so much good and yet also so much bad? In the book of Romans, the apostle Paul reminds us of the constant pull of fallen human nature; the truth is that for all of us there exists a dichotomy between doing good and doing bad. Speaking personally, in a way to which I am sure all of us can relate, Paul says: 'For in my inner being I delight in God's law; but I see another law at work in the members of my body, waging war against the law of my mind and making me a prisoner of the law of sin at work within my members' (Rom. 7:22–23). The reality is that whilst we are '… fearfully and wonderfully made' (Psa. 139:14) by the Divine Designer, mankind's decision to operate in independence from God at the beginning of time (Gen. 3:1–7) marred our original design.

With the help of the *Designed for Living* workbook we are going to explore who God intended us to be, who we are as a result of brokenness in the world and how we can reach the potential God has for us through personal insight, surrender and implementing change. James Mallory and Stanley C. Baldwin, in their book, *Kink and I: A Psychiatrist's Guide to Untwisted Living* say: 'A person can never understand why he behaves the way he does, nor the importance and implications of his behaviour until he understands who and what he is.'[1]

Let's begin by considering the design which went into our original creation (Gen. 1:26–27) and the effects of the Fall on our design. In the first three chapters of Genesis we see that:

1. God is relational (Father, Son and Holy Spirit) and, because we
    are made in His image, we were also designed to be relational.
    Firstly to relate to God, our Maker, and secondly, to other people.

2. God is spirit (see also John 4:24) and we too possess an immortal
    spirit (which is what distinguishes us from the rest of creation).
    The spirit is the invisible part of us by which we perceive, reflect,
    feel, desire etc.

    Because God is spirit and relational, He has the capacity to think,
    feel and choose. We reflect Him in each of these areas as we,
    too, have these capacities. However God, being holy and without
    sin, operates in perfection in all these areas. Prior to the Fall the
    hearts of Adam and Eve were inclined towards righteousness.
    Using the metaphor of a three-legged stool, as they related to
    God there existed a total sense of:

    - **security** (belonging and attachment,
      with no fear of rejection)
    - **self-worth** (personal value and self-esteem)
    - **significance** (meaning and purpose and
      that one's life counts)

However, sin devastated mankind's image; Eve, in reaching for more security and independence, found insecurity. She not only lost her innocence, she brought shame to her husband. Her secure and serene world vanished; for the first time she knew fear. Adam and Eve became spiritually and socially separated from each other. They rebelled against their Creator, and as a consequence of their sin they were disconnected from God. As a result, every area of human functioning was impacted and we live with the negative effects today. If we can understand life as God intended and the effects of our broken relationship with Him, then we can know the power of restoration and its implications on our worth, value and femininity. We will be considering these in turn.

Made in God's image, we are longing, thinking, choosing and feeling beings (in physical form), but as a result of the shattered image, we have become:

- **longing** beings controlled by the pain of our unmet longings which only God can meet
- **thinking** beings whose beliefs arise out of our unmet longings and determine our feelings
- **choosing** beings whose will does not operate in isolation and is driven by our longings
- **feeling** beings whose emotions are intensified by our beliefs and drive our choices
- **physical** beings whose bodies are affected by all aspects of our functioning and are subject to decay

Over the next seven sessions we will explore all the above areas of human functioning, how these can disrupt our living as children of God and as women of destiny, and how we can work at taking steps towards greater maturity.

Explore the Bible

Read Genesis 1–3: The story of creation.

Consider how different life would be now had Adam and Eve not chosen independence from God. List any differences that come to mind.

 # Ask yourself

- We live in an age where society affirms labels, be it a maker of a product or a description of a person; in addition we all have the tendency to label both ourselves and other people. The labels can be positive ('I'm a cheerful person'), negative ('I'm a failure') or simply descriptive ('I'm a hard-working mum'). Many of the labels we place on ourselves come out of our state of being fallen or involve comparing ourselves negatively with others.

   What labels have you given yourself over the years?

- As Christians we bear one label, a designer label, not a cheap copy; we bear the label of being a child of God made in the image of God (Gen. 1:27).

   Setting aside the labels you have given yourself, can you choose to keep central to your life the most important label: 'I am a child of God made in His image'? Why might you find this difficult?

- To understand who we are and the potential we have, we must first understand who God is and what He is like.

Read the following verses: Isaiah 30:18; Psalm 145:9; Numbers 14:18; Psalm 36:6; Ephesians 2:4; James 1:17; Psalm 89:1; Deuteronomy 32:4.
What do these verses tell you about the nature of God?

As we are made in the image of God, what do they also tell you about how we can choose to act as children of God?

. . . .

Listen to others

I've been a Christian for 27 years, but the image of the three-legged stool (illustrating security, self-worth and significance) has been one of the most helpful concepts in understanding my relationship to Christ. I realised that I'd often put my husband or family in place of God and that I'd sought to satisfy my deep thirsts and longings in people and places, when only God could really fill them. In facing this, I've been able to grasp the incredible depth of God's love and grace for me and to turn afresh to Him, repent of my independence and offer myself fully again to Him. It has been incredibly liberating and redeeming.

During this time of understanding how each area of our function is connected to the other, by applying what I have learned and through allowing God to develop the fruits of the Spirit in me, I have received both physical and emotional healing from the scars of the past. Consequently I feel that I have been released to fulfil my destiny and live more fully in God's world in God's way.

Fiona

Take it deeper

In Genesis 3 we read of how the eyes of Adam and Eve 'were opened' after eating the fruit. Realising that they were naked, they sewed fig leaves together and made coverings for themselves. However, their feelings of nakedness did not merely concern their physical unclothed state but also their sense of exposure before God (of whom they'd previously been unafraid and in whose presence they'd felt no shame). Life as God intended included complete openness with Him, without the need to hide or withdraw at any time.

Reflect

What sorts of things tend to result in you hiding from God or not communicating with Him as easily as you usually do?

How does this manifest itself?

In what way is your relationship with others and yourself affected?

Prayer

Father, thank You that I am fearfully and wonderfully made; not only am I made with such intricate detail but I am made in Your image, bearing a part of who You are – that's awesome!

SUGGESTED PRAYER THEMES
- Openness with God.
- Letting go of labelling ourselves.

Creative Ideas

Tools needed:

1. Credit card size pieces of paper/card on which different words are written
2. Enough blank cards for everyone in the group
3. Coloured pens

Make lots of little cards (enough for everyone in the group to have at least three each) on which is written either a positive or negative descriptive word, eg friendly, warm, compassionate, grumpy, gentle, insensitive, intelligent, lazy. You can have repeat cards.

Cont'd

During the first 'Ask Yourself' section, place all the cards with the words on face down on a table. Ask each person to take several cards. When the group is ready to look at the words on their cards, ask them to discuss whether the words are an accurate description of themselves.

During the second 'Ask Yourself' section, hand out the blank cards and ask everyone to write down the words: 'I am a child of God made in His image', to read it out loud as a means of owning the truth about themselves – and to keep the card as a reminder.

 Have a smile

At Sunday School children were being taught how God created everything, including human beings. Little Johnny, a child in the kindergarten class, seemed especially intent when they told him how Eve was created out of one of Adam's ribs. Later in the week his mother noticed him lying as though he were ill and said, 'Johnny, what is the matter?'

Little Johnny responded, 'I have a pain in my side. I think I'm going to have a wife!'*

---

1   James Mallory and Stanley C. Baldwin, *Kink and I: A Psychiatrist's Guide to Untwisted Living*, (Wheaton, Illinois: Scripture Press Publications, 1973).

*   See copyright page.

Hungry for something

There is more hunger for love and appreciation in this world than for bread.

(Mother Teresa)

We are longing beings and there's no mistaking the fact that we are driven by, and often conduct our lives in response to, our emotional hunger and spiritual thirst. When we examine our hearts closely it is clear that actually we all:

- long for something
- are controlled by what we long for
- encounter personal problems when our longings are not met.

We may not realise it but we live life in a parched state, which is a legacy from the Fall. Ever since Adam and Eve chose independence, mankind has been living with an emptiness of unmet needs. True satisfaction only comes in recognising the origins of our emptiness and choosing to turn to our Maker for fulfilment. The psalmist sums it up for us in his words: 'My soul thirsts for God, for the living God' (Psa. 42:2).

Following on from the last session, when we looked at the impact of the Fall, we see that attributes became needs and what had previously been a source of great satisfaction became a source of frustration, deep longings and self-focused attempts at gratification. Having moved out of their close relationship with God, Adam and Eve could no longer experience the high degree of security, self-worth and significance for which they had been created and instead experienced **insecurity, inferiority** and **insignificance**. We have carried the consequences, a craving for security, worth and significance, ever since.

As children, much of our need for security, self-worth and significance is met, at a natural level, through our parents or those who nurture us, but because all of us (to a lesser or greater degree) are parented by imperfect parents, we carry into adulthood distortions in thinking about ourselves and insecurities concerning our interactions with others. One of the long-term effects of the Fall has been low self-esteem. This is a common problem, particularly amongst women, worsened by the fact that society often rates personal value by performance, achievement and body image. Some women wear their doubts about themselves on their sleeve; others compensate by appearing to be highly competent but their deceptive appearance hides a multitude of insecurities.

However we come across, at the core of our being we are desperate to assuage the empty ache inside. The world offers us, amongst other things, sex, success, food or alcohol as a panacea. If we are not willing to acknowledge our deep longings and the pain of unmet needs, we will live on the surface of life and come to believe that anything can satisfy. It is very humbling to recognise the thirst that only God can satisfy; and the more we allow God to meet our needs, the deeper He can take us into relationship with Him.

In relation to our emotional and spiritual appetites, C.S. Lewis reminds us that we have the tendency to settle for less than the best and to reduce our longings to the minimum; in effect we become happy to have the starter and miss out on the banquet: '... Our Lord finds our desires not too strong, but too weak. We are half-hearted creatures, fooling about with drink and sex and ambition when infinite joy is offered us, like an innocent child who wants to go on making mud pies in a slum because he cannot imagine what is meant by the offer of a holiday at the sea. We are far too easily pleased'.[1]

As a consequence of original sin, we now live with the capacity for happiness but the drivenness to fill it with things that don't fully satisfy. The prophet Jeremiah, speaking of how the Israelites had done the same in turning to idols rather than to the Living God, says:

'My people have committed two sins: They have forsaken me, the spring of living water, and have dug their own cisterns, broken cisterns that cannot hold water.'

Jer. 2:13

The people of Israel turned from Him, the spring of living water, and dug their own dirty cisterns, to drink their own water; they turned a blind eye to the God who was their object of worship and source of satisfaction and made idols their objects of worship and focus of happiness.

What is important to note is that God does not condemn the people for their thirsts and their needs (just as He doesn't condemn us for our needs); rather He condemns them for rejecting His provision and making an independent decision about what will meet their needs. When we attempt to make life work outside of God and fill our lives with possessions, obsessions and shallow sources of comfort and joy, we dig for ourselves broken cisterns. It may sound harsh, but anything we turn to in order to provide worth and value, above God, is actually a form of *idolatry*. We develop strategies and allow other people and things to occupy our attention. We are motivated, albeit subconsciously, to find our identity and source of life in ways other than through God.

In order to feel secure and worthwhile as women we have a tendency to rely on the following: what other people think of us, fashion, image, family, ministry, homes, success, cars etc. These can too easily be placed above our relationship with God and therefore become forms of idolatry. There is nothing wrong in wanting to be a successful businesswoman, good mother, caring friend, top artist – but not one of these is an end in itself. They cannot replace our need to find our value in Christ.

Explore the Bible

Read Isaiah 44:14–17

This is the story of a man who plants a tree in a forest. He lets it grow, then, at the right time, he cuts down the tree ...

> *Half of the wood he burns in the fire; over it he prepares his meal, he roasts his meat and eats his fill. He also warms himself and says, 'Ah! I am warm; I see the fire.' From the rest he makes a god, his idol; he bows down to it and worships. He prays to it and says, 'Save me; you are my god'*
>
> *Isa. 44:16–17*

'Silly man!' you may say. But hang on – note that he begins by using the wood for its rightful purpose: for cooking his meal and for warming himself. But he goes a step further and makes the wood into something that he worships. He worships the thing rather than the Creator/giver of the thing.

Do we do this in our own lives? What do we tend to turn into idols?

Read John 4:1–26

The woman at the well was there to draw water. She had also dug another well in her life, eg that of relying on men to try to meet her needs in the ways she thought would be effective. Jesus offered her living water which would totally quench the thirst in her soul. Jesus is offering *us* that same living water.

Ask yourself

- Men and women tend to vary in the priority they would place on the three inner needs.

   As a woman, what do you find yourself longing for most?

   For *you*, which would you describe as being the most significant driving force behind 'feeling OK': security, significance or self-worth?

- Victor Hugo once said: 'The supreme happiness of life is the conviction that we are loved.'

   How does the love of God vary from the love of mankind?

Listen to others

I was brought up in an atheist family. The headmaster of my junior school was a Jewish rabbi and my other teachers were virtually all atheists.

I was taught most vigorously at my grammar school (and was also very strongly encouraged by my family) to get my 'fulfilment' in life through my future career. The school told us over and over that our lives would be ruined if we didn't get at least eight 'O levels'; I got thirteen and sought to get my needs met in my work.

It was a total revelation to me to realise that it was idolatrous to get my needs for security, significance and self-worth met by my job. I had been to church for about fourteen years (well-known churches too) and had never been taught about what idolatry actually was.

I radically repented of my idolatrous attitude and for about three months afterwards had supernatural peace, joy and my own 'mini revival'. It impacted those close to me too: my mother-in-law telephoned me not long afterwards and said that she had felt led to get on a bus and get off wherever God told her to. She got off outside a church where an evangelistic service was being held and made a commitment to Christ.

Anne

◪ Take it deeper

- We were built and designed for a relationship with God and, however good the relationship has been with our parents and significant others, it is not enough to meet the deep needs of our spirit. Being made in the image of God, our identity is to be found in Him. In Him dwells all the fullness of the Godhead in bodily form (Col. 2:9–10) and we are each complete in Him.

  In addition to significance, security and self-worth, do you seek to find a *sense of identity* in things other than God? If so, in what?

  In what way would you say that your own attempts to fill core needs let you down?

Prayer

Father, I realise that my own attempts at generating significance, value, security and identity are so empty and futile in comparison with what You have given me. Help me to embrace all You have made me to be and all You have given me – that I may live in the fullness of satisfaction that only You can provide. Amen.

SUGGESTED PRAYER THEMES

- Recognising God as the One able to meet our needs and the giver of unconditional love.
- Recognising that making anything or anyone a higher priority than God is a form of idolatry.

Creative Ideas

Tools needed:

1. Large (A3) size piece of paper or card
2. Scissors
3. Glue

Bring to the session (or ask the group to bring) images from magazines or the internet that are presented as sources of security, significance and self-worth, particularly to women. This could be linked to body image, fashion, make-up, ideal home, money, pets, cars or, in conjunction with careers, achievement, relationships etc.

Cont'd

> At the start of the first 'Ask Yourself' section stick the images at random onto the card to create a collage out of the various images people have brought to the session. The aim of this is to create a picture which highlights where women so often find their security and worth.

Have a smile

A Sunday School teacher asked her class: 'If Jesus walked into this room right now, what would you do?'

One little girl thought about it and replied: 'I would walk up behind Him, tap Him on the shoulder and when He turned round, I would smile, give Him a Bible and say, "This is your life!"'**

---

1   C.S. Lewis, *The Weight of Glory* (Grand Rapids: William B. Eerdmans Publishing Co., 1965) p.2. Copyright © C.S. Lewis Pte Ltd 1949. Extract printed by permission.

**   See copyright page.

Ways we hold back

True repentance has a double aspect. It looks upon things past with a weeping eye, and upon the future with a watchful eye.

(Robert Smith)

The German poet, dramatist and novelist, Johann Wolfgang Von Goethe (1749–1832), once said: 'People do not mind their faults being spread out before them, but they become impatient if called on to give them up.' We saw in the last session how we so easily turn to things other than God for the fulfilment of our needs when, in fact, God Himself offers us all we require. Allowing ourselves to face the truth that we all try to build our own cisterns (sources of satisfaction) is one thing, but actually *letting go* of those cisterns and allowing God to meet our needs is another.

Typically, we either deny that we have deep needs or we build defences in order to maintain our own means of meeting those needs. We then wonder why we live with a sense of shifting security and variable worth, which are vulnerable to the inconsistencies of other people and life circumstances.

When we are in defensive or protective mode we tend to do one of the following with our unmet longings:

- **transfer** them from a need for relationship with God to a need for attention and affirmation from other people
- **redirect** them (and instead meet our needs through success or material possessions)
- **anaesthetise** them (through activities, addictions, obsessions and 'buying sprees')

- **compensate** for them (through career, achievement, status and the roles or masks we take on)

Through these and other means we hold back both from allowing God to be in control and from making changes in our lives. We may even convince ourselves that there is little difference between God's ways and our ways. However, the book of Isaiah and the proverbs of Solomon give a clear message about the difference between God's ways and our ways:

> 'For my thoughts are not your thoughts, neither are your ways my ways,' declares the LORD.
>
> Isa. 55:8

> Trust in the LORD with all your heart and lean not on your own understanding ...
>
> Prov. 3:5

When writing to the Romans the apostle Paul sums up succinctly the nature of what mankind does that is offensive to God: 'They exchanged the truth of God for a lie, and worshipped and served created things rather than the Creator ...' (Rom. 1:25). We may not seem as rebellious as the people of whom Paul spoke, but nevertheless we so easily exchange the truth for something less. Satan's ploy is to undermine our trust in God through doubt and distorted thinking and to lead us to believe we are in the right.

The realisation that *we* conduct our lives and that God doesn't like this may sound somewhat depressing; the good news is that we can, with humility, recognise how we displace God, say we are sorry and change our ways. In other words, we can repent. First, however, we need to make sure we understand what repentance really is: it is not regret, which is feeling sorry for oneself; it is not remorse, which eats into the heart, rather than seeking a new heart. The Greek word for repentance is *metanoia*, which means *change of mind*. In the biblical context repentance is a *change of mind about where life is found* or as Thomas J. Watson Sr. once said: 'Repentance is a grace of God's Spirit whereby a sinner is inwardly humbled and visibly reformed.' The main focus of our repentance is threefold:

i.   our failure to trust God and His love for us

ii. our unwillingness to believe His evaluation of our worth

iii. our refusal to see meaning or purpose in our lives.

Repentance is coming to God for forgiveness, but to understand the power of God's forgiveness we must first understand the ugliness of our own sin. Also, if we don't understand forgiveness from God then it is difficult to forgive other people when we are offended or have been wronged. The greatest dynamic for positive change and personal growth is our relationship with God. The only way to keep that relationship fresh is to live with a heart that is willing to repent when we allow anything or anyone else to take the place of God in the meeting of our deepest needs.

Explore the Bible

Read 2 Corinthians 7:10–11; Acts 26:9–23; Hosea 14:1–3

What do you learn about God's character through these three readings?

Read Ephesians 2:1–7

Why did the members of the church at Ephesus need to repent?

Ask yourself

- Paul had a dramatic conversion which would have resulted in a complete change in attitude towards himself and other people, as well as in a letting go of certain defences and actions.

  What do you envisage may have gone through Paul's mind at the time of his 'Damascus Road experience'? What emotions might he have felt?

- The changes that Paul made to his lifestyle and way of treating others were as a direct consequence of a revelation of Jesus.

  What changes might God be asking you to make at this point in your life? Do you need to pray for a fresh revelation of Jesus in order to make genuine, lasting changes?

Listen to others

I would frequently say 'Sorry' to God for things I had done that I knew weren't right, but the word 'repentance' always sounded a bit 'heavy' – and I would shy away from it. It wasn't until I really grasped how much God loves me and until, one day, I realised how anything I do outside of trusting Him displaces Him from the centre of my life that I really understood what it meant to repent. My words were more than simply saying 'Sorry'; I had a deep awakening of how, in so many areas of my life, I had failed to trust Him and how I had desired my way more than His way. I knew that my words of repentance had to be followed by a change in me; taking action so that my life would be visibly different. It's transformed the way I see repentance – it brings freedom and hope.

Sarah

Take it deeper

- We have seen how our tendency as human beings is either to deny our needs or to cover them up.

  Which would you say you tend to do the most: cover up, numb, fill or ignore your inner hunger?

What defence mechanisms and behaviours do you tend to use to feel better about yourself? (Do you intellectualise, joke, act the victim, manipulate, blame others, rescue others, buy people's affection with gifts or prove yourself by success?)

Prayer

Heavenly Father, forgive me, I pray, for so foolishly trying to meet my needs in my own way when I see that You and You alone are to be my supply. I repent of my self-sufficiency and my self-centredness [identify any other sins that need to be brought before God]. I ask You now for Your forgiveness for my stubborn and arrogant refusal to trust You with my needs for security, self-worth and significance. Help me, Lord Jesus, from now on to turn in daily dependence and to draw from You, the uniquely sufficient God, all I need to bring me security, value and fulfilment in life. In Christ's name I pray, Amen.

SUGGESTED PRAYER THEMES

- Asking forgiveness for not loving God with all our heart, mind, will and emotion.
- Asking forgiveness for not loving others in the way in which God calls us to.

Creative Ideas

Tools needed:

1. A box with a slot (like a letter box, such as an empty tissue box) or a cross and candle
2. Scrap paper and pens

During the 'Prayer themes' section, give people the opportunity to take a small piece of paper and write down what they would like to repent of. They can then post it into the box or place it at the foot of the cross. At the end of the session what is on the pieces of paper can be handed over symbolically to God in a collective prayer and the papers can be disposed of, without reading them, by the group leader.

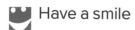 Have a smile

A Sunday School teacher was discussing the Ten Commandments with her five- and six-year-olds. After explaining the commandment to 'Honour thy father and mother', she asked, 'Is there a commandment that teaches us how to treat our brothers and sisters?'

One little boy replied, 'Thou shalt not kill.'*

* See copyright page.

PART 2 –
Restoring our divine image

Affirming our value

Until you make peace with who you are, you'll never be content with what you have.

(Doris Mortman)

In the last session we explored how all of us have, at some stage, placed our security, significance and self-worth in things other than God and have consequently been guilty of *idolatry*. God declares: 'You shall have no other gods before me' (Deut. 5:7). Recognition and repentance of this is the most significant step we can take in our journey towards maturity. When we move *ourselves* out of the driving seat, *God* can move in – and the foundation for our whole functioning changes.

In the first session we said that whilst we are '… fearfully and wonderfully made' (Psa. 139:14) by the Divine Designer, mankind's decision to operate in independence from God at the beginning of time (Gen. 3:1–7) marred our original design. As women we have embraced that sense of being marred and so easily carry not only the results of sin in our lives, but add to that our own perception of not being quite good enough. We try to feel good about ourselves often by bettering our body (or desiring to better our body – but never quite making it). Let's face it: women are renowned for comfort eating, dieting, exercising to burn off calories, trying new fads, following fashion, changing hairstyles and even carrying out more drastic measures in an attempt to feel better about themselves. Does it really work? 'It is estimated that the diet industry alone is worth anywhere between 40 to 100 billion US dollars a year selling temporary weight loss (90–95% of dieters regain the lost weight).'[1] Despite these facts, women carry on following the same trends.

It's not that healthy weight control, fashion and making the most of our looks is wrong, but it is all too easy to place our value on these things and, even when near perfection is attained, still feel not good enough! In recognising that we have put other things in place of God or placed a lack of value on ourselves, we become aware of the choice we have to change our perception and embrace what God says about us. Failing to do so will have negative effects – not just on ourselves but on others too. In the words of Sydney J. Harris, it is incredible how many people 'go through life without ever recognising that their feelings toward other people are largely determined by their feelings toward themselves, and if you're not comfortable within yourself, you can't be comfortable with others'.

We are created in the image of God; a pretty awesome fact when you consider that He is the Creator of the whole universe. Being created in God's image means that we are 'image bearers'; what is the image we bear? Amongst other things, the Bible describes God as righteous, merciful, loving, wise, joyful, majestic, trustworthy, radiant, pure, compassionate ... Due to the fact that we are created in the image of God, we bear something of His character; we are not perfect in these characteristics (because our inner and outer beauty have been marred as a result of the Fall), but we do have the capacity to reflect something of God. Through the work of the Holy Spirit in our lives, and as we go on surrendering ourselves to Christ, the character of God is made manifest.

Your beauty should not come from outward adornment,
such as braided hair and the wearing of gold jewellery and
fine clothes. Instead, it should be that of your inner

self, the unfading beauty of a gentle and quiet spirit, which is of great worth in God's sight.

1 Pet. 3:3–4

Being made in God's image and chosen by Him we are, despite our sin and disobedience, valuable to Him. Our value is not based on how we look or on what we do, but on *who we are in Christ,* that *we are created in God's image,* and *each of us is loved unconditionally by Him.* We cannot add to our worth; nor can we take anything away from it. It is not of our making: it is God's gift to us as His dearly beloved children. We see clearly just how much God loves us when we look at the cross and understand that God sent His own Son to restore our relationship with Him.

For God so loved the world that he gave his one and only Son, that whoever believes in him shall not perish but have eternal life'.

John 3:16

The Bible tells us much about our identity, worth and value which we inherit as children of God when we receive Jesus as Lord of our lives. We are accepted, secure and significant, as the following scriptures reveal.

- We belong to God – 1 Corinthians 6:19–20
- We are adopted as His children – Galatians 4:5–6
- Our sins have been forgiven – Colossians 1:13–14
- We are free from condemnation – Romans 8:1–2
- Nothing can separate us from the love of God – Romans 8:31–39

- We are citizens of heaven – Philippians 3:20
- We are God's temple – 1 Corinthians 3:16; 6:19
- We are God's workmanship – Ephesians 2:10
- We have been chosen to bear fruit – John 15:16

Explore the Bible

Read Psalm 139

It can sometimes be helpful to read familiar passages in a different translation. Doing so often brings out aspects of the reading which you may have not fully grasped or helps you to see things from a different perspective. Try reading Psalm 139 in *The Message* or The New Living Translation.

Ask yourself

- Bearing in mind that you are made in the image of the Almighty God:

  In what ways do you tend to belittle God's creation (given that we all have times when we fail to embrace and affirm our true value)?

How can you affirm your value without being proud? God has commanded us to 'love [our] neighbour as [ourself]' (Lev. 19:18; Matt. 19:19; Gal. 5:14).

What do the following proverbs tell you about how you should act towards both yourself and others?

- Proverbs 3:3; 12:18; 28:13; 10:9; 16:32; 29:23

· ·

Listen to others

When I hit my teens I began to struggle with low self-worth. I'd had quite a troubled childhood and had never been particularly happy, but by the time I was about fourteen I suffered from depression and self-loathing. Just before my twentieth birthday I became a Christian. At first, I felt differently about myself, but the old way of judging and perceiving myself soon stepped in again. I was always comparing myself to others and was very conscious of how I looked. I only felt 'good enough' if people commented on me looking nice or they wanted to spend time with me. I didn't know what I liked and didn't like and would constantly change my clothes, hairstyle etc.

I'd heard phrases like: 'You're a child of God' and 'God loves you', over and over again, but they had little impact on me because I always undermined the words with my own negative thoughts towards myself. One day, after learning more about what it really means to be taken from the kingdom of darkness to the kingdom of light and to be rooted in Christ and be a part of His inheritance, I had a revelation that I don't have to feel bad about myself – I am of incredible worth, not through trying to 'better' myself but because I have been given all I need by God. My whole outlook on life has changed.

Sally

Take it deeper

- Josh McDowell once said, 'A healthy self-esteem is seeing your-self as God sees you – no more and no less',[2] but many women struggle to do this.

What stops you believing what the Bible says about you?

What changes can you make to allow the truth to impact you more deeply?

Prayer

Father, the most important person for me to look to as a reflection of my value is You. Where I hold wrong perceptions and judge myself according to unhelpful standards and attitudes, I ask that You do a mighty work. Show me where my beliefs that hinder me affirming my value have come from and open my eyes to see Your love for me – so that I may accept myself and, in doing so, love others as myself.

SUGGESTED PRAYER THEMES

- Give thanks to God for His unconditional, overwhelming, forgiving love.
- Lay down wrong concepts of yourself, asking for God's forgiveness.
- Affirm who you are in Christ.

Creative Ideas

Tools needed:

1. CD player
2. Passage from a book or print-out from the internet

At the start of the time of prayer play a song which speaks of God's love for us as His children, for example Matt Redman's song, 'The Father's Song' (Kingsway, © 2000 Thankyou Music).

Read a poem or piece of prose which reinforces how much we, as God's children, mean to Him.

 Have a smile

A little girl was sitting on her grandfather's lap as he read her a bedtime story. From time to time, she would take her eyes off the book and reach up to touch his wrinkled cheek. She was alternately stroking her own cheek, then his again. Finally she spoke up, 'Grandpa, did God make you?'

'Yes, sweetheart,' he answered, 'God made me a long time ago.'

'Oh,' she paused, 'Grandpa, did God make me too?'

'Yes, indeed, honey,' he said, 'God made you just a little while ago.'

Feeling their respective faces again, she observed, 'God's getting better at it, isn't He?'*

---

1 '*The diet business: Banking on failure.*' (BBC News World Edition, 5 Feb 2003), http://news.bbc.co.uk/2/hi/business/2725943.stm

2 Josh Mc Dowell, *His Image, My Image* (Carlisle: Authentic Media, 2005).

* See copyright page.

Recognising our behaviour

It is not only what we do, but also what we do not do, for which we are accountable.

(Molière)

We were created by God to operate with free will; with the capacity to make choices. It may not always feel like it, but we have a choice as to how we respond to our inner needs and where we place our trust.

We are longing beings and we are all controlled by what we long for. We will strive, work hard, do everything we can to satisfy the longings of our soul. As people who are longing for security, significance and self-worth, we are powerfully motivated to have those needs met. The pain of those unmet longings drives us to find a way to meet them. Whatever we believe will meet those needs becomes *our goal*, whether we are aware of having made a choice or not at the time.

Some psychologists advocate that the way we behave today is influenced by what has happened in our past, hence it is the past more than the present which causes us to behave in the way we do. Of course there is truth in this, but it doesn't mean that we are not responsible for our behaviour and are merely being driven by the past, with no control. All of us emerge from our childhood with custom-designed strategies for keeping our rational lives, at least, moderately pain-free and somehow manageable. We have directed our energy towards doing whatever will work to keep us from sadness and to feel in control.

In order to understand our behaviour and be restored we must realise that we are not merely victims of circumstance but we are people with God-given volition (capacity for choice). As such, we need to consider what goal our behaviour is trying to achieve, bearing in mind that our beliefs dictate our goals.

Let's look at a couple of examples:

1. If we believe that we will be accepted and loved if we look good, our goal will be to be admired through our external appearance, in the hope of gaining the sense of acceptance and unconditional love for which we thirst.
2. If we believe that people will think well of us if we are hospitable and open our homes to them, our goal will be to serve people in our homes, in order to earn worth in their eyes and prove to ourselves and others that we have value.

It's not that wanting to look good, be hospitable etc. are bad in themselves, but rather that they cannot be the true source of our satisfaction and they will never fully meet our needs. If we look to having these in our lives as our source of worth, then their absence will affect both our value and security. Our true sense of worth comes from God and our goal is to honour Him. In that respect any goal we set up where we are not putting God at the centre of our lives and trusting in Him for our worth can be classed as a *wrong goal*.

Taking responsibility for our wrong goals is an important step in establishing security in our lives. When we are feeling insecure, we can choose God as our source of security. When we are feeling inferior, we can choose God as the source of our self-worth. When we are feeling insignificant, we can choose God as the source of our significance. These things may not come naturally, but we *can choose* them.

 # Explore the Bible

Read and discuss Romans 7:14–8:11

Read 2 Corinthians 5:9

What goal can we choose to pursue that can never be blocked, unreachable or uncertain?

 # Ask yourself

- The energy, power and 'drivenness' behind our behaviour is most often the pain of our unmet needs. The pain of feeling insecure, inferior and insignificant, influenced by our thinking, drives us to pursue certain goals and make the choices we do.

  When do you feel secure and when might you feel insecure?

How does your behaviour tie in with this?

What belief might be behind the behaviour you carry out?

Listen to others

I've always been very indecisive and, despite numerous attempts, have found it very difficult to get over this. The only thing that eventually made a difference was realising what purpose my indecision was serving. I held a belief that in order to feel good about myself I had to be liked by everyone all the time. Subconsciously, I had set up the goal to please people and my indecision was because I had to discover what would most please the other person. I've been challenging myself over this and finding the freedom to be myself – and, I have to say, it's really liberating!

Jane

Take it deeper

- We can become very dependent upon our wrong goals, to the point that we feel we *must* have them in order to survive. This sets up a *demand* within us and we will manipulate situations and people in order to achieve our goal. Our goals can even become our idols.

  Can you think of a situation where the pain of an unmet need was so great that you manipulated a person or a situation in order to achieve your goal to feel good about yourself (even if at the time you didn't realise it).

  As a result of the teaching we have been exploring, how could you have responded to your needs differently?

Prayer

Father, as I spend this time studying these truths, I ask that You would bring to mind different times and situations where I have chosen to make demands or I have manipulated and controlled people and situations in order to get my own needs met. I repent of these and ask for Your forgiveness. Give me the courage to trust You with my deepest needs and to not use other people inappropriately. Amen.

> ### *Prayer of Serenity*
> *God grant me the serenity*
> *to accept the things I cannot change;*
> *courage to change the things I can;*
> *and wisdom to know the difference.*
>
> (Attributed to Reinhold Neibuhr)

We like this adaptation of the prayer:

> *God grant me the serenity*
> *to accept the people I cannot change;*
> *courage to change the person I can;*
> *and wisdom to know it's me.*

SUGGESTED PRAYER THEMES

- Acknowledgement of pain and the way we tend to respond to it.
- Giving thanks that Jesus, our High Priest, is able to sympathise with our weaknesses because He has been tempted in every way, but without sin (Heb. 4:15).

Creative Ideas

Instructions:

1. The group divides into pairs
2. The pairs move around to give some personal space

Our behaviour or actions can affect others. Throughout this exercise make note of how your partner's behaviour affects how you feel or think.

Person A: You desire to have a conversation with a friend and are in need of feeling understood and heard. Talk to your partner about the hard day you have had or the difficult circumstances in which you find yourself at the moment.

Person B: You are preoccupied, not making eye contact, self-focused or obsessed with something in your own life. You fail to really listen to what your friend is saying and are determined to get your own points of view across.

Swap roles and do the exercise again, but this time:

Person A: You have some good news and are excited.

Person B: You are feeling melancholic, negative, depressed and disinterested.

Feed back to the group the effect the other person's behaviour and words had on you.

Have a smile

A kindergarten teacher was observing her classroom of children while they were drawing. She would occasionally walk around to see each child's work.

As she got to one little girl who was working diligently, she asked what the drawing was.

The girl replied, 'I'm drawing God.'

The teacher paused and said, 'But no one knows what God looks like.'

Without looking up from her drawing, the girl replied, 'They will in a minute.'*

---

*   See copyright page.

Directing our thoughts

There are no hopeless situations; there are only people who have grown hopeless about them.

(Clare Boothe Luce)

We have looked at how our unmet needs drive us to make choices to pursue wrong goals. The reason we pursue those goals also has to do with our underlying thinking. Behaviour begins with a thought; thoughts lead to feelings; and feelings to decisions and actions.

Thoughts ⟶ Feelings ⟶ Decisions ⟶ Actions

Being made in God's image we have the capacity to think, although our thoughts are very different from His thoughts. '"For my thoughts are not your thoughts, neither are your ways my ways," declares the LORD' (Isa. 55:8). A consequence of the Fall is that our thinking and judgments are marred; we are predisposed to selfish and self-seeking thinking, geared towards our own state of comfort. Though we may believe God's truth, we draw our own irrational conclusions to which we hold fast; these conclusions are often based on negative past experiences. The sooner we can identify our wrong (often irrational) beliefs the sooner we can free ourselves from the powerful effect they have on our lives, because they will affect our emotions and behaviour negatively. The enemy will also speak into our minds to draw our thinking away from God and cause doubt.

Not only does the enemy speak into our minds but we also speak to ourselves. Research has shown that we talk to ourselves (self-talk) at a rate of around 1,300 words per minute. Negative words result in negative emotions, so if our self-talk is irrational and not based on the Truth then we will feel pretty lousy!

Irrational beliefs, amongst other things, may have one of the following characteristics associated with them:

1. Demandingness: key words would be: *ought, should, must*
2. 'Awfulising': key words would be: *terrible, awful, unbearable*
3. Self-devaluation: key words would be: *failure, useless, undeserving*

We carry some beliefs deep inside us and, when we experience strong negative emotions, we do not realise that our beliefs are responsible for the way we feel. These beliefs may be unconscious and irrational. As long as we hold on to these irrational beliefs they will affect the way we respond to life, 'For as he thinks in his heart, so *is* he' (Prov. 23:7a, NKJV, our emphasis); hence it is important to challenge and replace these irrational beliefs with the Truth.

To function effectively our minds must be renewed. Paul, in his letter to the Romans, writes: 'Do not conform any longer to the pattern of this world, but be transformed by the renewing of your mind. Then you will be able to test and approve what God's will is – his good, pleasing and perfect will' (Rom. 12:2). No longer being conformed to this world means that we must challenge our thinking that is not according to biblical principles. To do this we must firstly recognise that we all have belief systems that essentially control our emotions.

Psychologist Albert Ellis explains the concept of how our belief systems affect us, in what is known as the 'ABC Theory of Emotion':

A = the *activating* event

B = the *belief* system

C = the *consequent* emotion

He says that it is not the event itself which results in the emotion but rather the belief system we hold about the event; in other words, our perception about the happening. CWR, in their Christian counselling training, take this concept a little further by saying that to deal with the faulty belief system we can add D (disputing the belief) and E (exchanging the belief for an accurate, scripturally based belief) to ABC.

A = the *activating* event

B = the *belief* system

C = the *consequent* emotion

D = the *disputing* of the wrong thinking

E = the scriptural *exchange*

We can challenge the wrong thoughts with what God's Word says:

> ... *whatever is true, whatever is noble, whatever is right, whatever is pure, whatever is lovely, whatever is admirable – if anything is excellent or praiseworthy – think about such things.*
>
> *Phil. 4:8*

Let's look at a situation which may occur in our lives and what the irrational belief (sometimes known as distorted thinking) may be:

A. You are walking down the road and see a friend you haven't seen for a while. You wave and she disappears into a shop.

B. Immediately, you think to yourself: 'She doesn't want to talk to me; I must have done something to upset her.'

C. You feel down and a bit anxious. You begin to 'awfulise'. You can't stop thinking about what you might have done to upset her and you feel pretty worthless. Then you think: 'Perhaps someone has said something unkind about me to her.'

D. You don't actually know why she didn't acknowledge you. The most obvious explanation is that she was preoccupied and didn't see you. Besides your worth isn't dependent on what she thinks of you.

E. I am loved by God and that is what gives me value (John 3:16). Therefore I do not need to fear rejection by anyone. I'll call my friend to catch up and let her know that I saw her in town.

Explore the Bible

Read Ephesians 4:17–32

How can you apply these verses to yourself rather than to your relationship with others?

Ask yourself

- Think of some situations of late which appear to result in you experiencing negative feelings.

What thought might be behind the feelings?

How can you correct that thought, based on biblical principles?

When corrected, what impact do you think it would have on your feelings?

· ·

Listen to others

The number of thoughts that go through our minds in a given day is astounding – we certainly would not be able to speak at the rate of our thoughts! Yet, are all our thoughts helpful? Do they reflect reality? The thought-catching module during a women's seminar helped me to distinguish between useful thoughts and thoughts that can provoke emotions that, in turn, can cause me to act in certain ways. In a sense we need to learn how to preach to ourselves. Why am I thinking that? What is behind this emotion? This is what I think – but what does Jesus think about this? What does His Word tell me is true? This way, catching our thoughts and really examining them can bring real life change – as most of our behaviours stem from a thought or belief which we have perhaps unwittingly internalised as true.

Jenny

· ·

◣ Take it deeper

- Behind most repetitive irrational thoughts lie past experiences, often uncomfortable or traumatic ones in childhood.

Make a list of negative words that may have been repeatedly spoken to you as a child.

In what way have these shaped your current thinking and interpretations?

Prayer

Father, I am so sorry for all the times and ways in which I have held irrational thoughts, believed untruths and allowed myself to dwell on that which is negative or destructive. I ask that You renew my thinking and help me to challenge it whenever it becomes distorted. I also pray that You would deliver and heal me from any past experiences that have influenced my thinking in an unhelpful way. Amen.

SUGGESTED PRAYER THEMES

- Ability to recognise irrational thoughts.
- Repentance for wrong thoughts about other people.
- Forgiveness for those who have hurt us.

Creative ideas

Tools needed:

1. An A4 piece of paper for every person in the group on which is photocopied the chart overleaf.
   (Include an example on the chart and space for people to add their own examples.)

During the 'Ask Yourself' section, hand out the chart overleaf and ask people to fill in one or two personal situations following the example given.

Suggest that they continue with this work over the weeks to come.

Event	Belief	Emotion	Dispute	Exchange

Have a smile

'Daddy, I want to ask you a question,' said little Bobby after his first day in Sunday School.

'Yes, Bobby, what is it?' his dad replied.

'The teacher was reading the Bible to us – all about the children of Israel building the temple, the children of Israel crossing the Red Sea, the children of Israel making sacrifices. Didn't the grown-ups do anything?'*

* See copyright page.

Channelling our emotions

When we learn to manage our emotions long enough to stop and shift our attention to the quieter message of the heart, we can gain a wider perspective on any situation, often saving ourselves from hurt, frustration and pain.

(Doc Childre & Howard Martin,
The HeartMath Solution)

As we have seen, behind our negative or troublesome emotions often lie negative thoughts; for instance, low self-esteem is something we *feel* but is actually caused by a *belief*. In order to reach our potential and live healthy emotional and spiritual lives as women, we need to learn not only to challenge those thoughts but to face, feel and process our emotions. Unacknowledged and unprocessed emotions result in numerous problems, affecting both our emotional and our physical wellbeing.

Our emotions so often threaten to overwhelm us, and many of our responses in life are emotionally driven, yet we so often deny how we feel. As Christian women, we can also hold wrong beliefs about emotions, believing, for example, 'I shouldn't get angry'. When such an emotion is present, we struggle to deal with it in a way that we think will be considered 'acceptable'. What we fail to realise is that what we think are 'Christian' ways of dealing with, for example, anger may not be Christlike at all. We may have chosen self-sufficiency over stridency, passivity rather than petulance, manipulation rather than outspokenness, emotional deadness as opposed to verbal abuse. But strategies that may be more socially acceptable are not necessarily Christ-reflecting or God-honouring; rather they do great damage to our own souls and the souls of those with whom we are interacting.

If we can understand our emotions we may feel less apprehensive of them. Emotions which cause struggles in life are really just 'warning signs'; red flags that shoot up to tell us that something needs to be addressed in our lives. If you were to see a little red flag go up you might ask yourself: 'What's up?' When we feel a certain way we need to ask ourselves the same question. Part of taking note of the red flag is recognising that, on the whole, our emotions fall into one of three main groups. Each group experienced will help to identify the type of goal we are pursuing.

- Anger and resentment indicate an undermined or *blocked* goal.
- Guilt and shame indicate an *unreachable* goal.
- Fear and anxiety indicate an *uncertain* goal.

Let's look at some typical situations which can arise in life.

1. Your friend arrives late to pick you up for a meeting and you feel *angry*. Your goal was *to be on time and to be seen as someone who is punctual*. By your friend not arriving on time your goal has been *blocked*.
2. You need to complete an essay for college and buy an outfit for your best friend's wedding, and you fail to complete the essay and feel guilty. You go into town first and run out of time to do the essay. Your goal was *to complete your work and buy an outfit by the end of the day*, but it was *unreachable* – you feel bad that you put shopping before study.

3. You go on a weekend course and soon after arriving feel very *anxious*. Your goal was *to feel a part of the group* and, as you look around, everyone seems different from you. You are *uncertain* as to whether you are going to fit in and cope with two full days of the course.

When we are faced with difficult emotions, it can be useful to ask ourselves a few key questions:

a) What is the thought that is energising this feeling? In other words, what might I be saying to myself about a particular situation which is resulting in me feeling a certain way?

b) If I work on the principle of: anger = a blocked goal; guilt = an unreachable goal; anxiety = an uncertain goal, what might my goal be?

c) What is preventing me from attaining my goal?

Generally, working out what lies behind an emotion brings understanding as to why we feel the way we do. It doesn't necessarily take away the feeling itself. Once we have some clarity over why an emotion might be present it can be useful to consider whether we are justified in feeling it. Try asking yourself: does the situation merit the feeling? If the answer is 'yes', then it is likely we need to feel and express the emotion (but in a way that is not destructive or undermining towards ourselves or others). If the answer is 'no', then it is likely we still have distorted thinking behind the feeling or it is exaggerated due to unresolved issues in the past.

Growing and developing as women requires us to deal with unresolved issues and traumas from the past. Dealing with complex issues goes beyond the remit of this workbook; however, understanding our emotions which arise out of here-and-now situations and learning to handle these well is a part of what we can work on during the course of our study together.

In learning about emotions, why not try to list as many different feelings as possible.[1] Besides being aware of the feelings and understanding their role, how do we express them appropriately? This is where people often get stuck. Finding appropriate avenues for expressing feelings is not always easy, but it is a part of our mental wellbeing and Christian responsibility. Many people resist their emotions because they fear the consequences of expressing feelings.

Some people use talking to express feelings; other people use various forms of creativity (writing, art, dance, drama etc). We all need to find what works best for us. Feelings often contain a lot of energy and a release comes when we allow that energy out – a good walk and talk with God, for instance! There are no right or wrong feelings, but in our expression of them we must be mindful that we don't contradict biblical principles.

Explore the Bible

Read John 11:1-44; Matthew 26:37–38; John 2:13–16

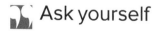

Ask yourself

- In the section 'Explore the Bible' we have just read several accounts where Jesus expressed emotion.

What do these passages tell you about how Jesus responded to His emotions?

Think of two situations where you experienced strong emotions: one where the emotion was justified; and the other where, perhaps, it was overexaggerated due to being fuelled by irrational thoughts and unresolved past issues.

Think of a time when you responded in a helpful way to your feelings and contrast it with a time when you responded in an unhelpful way.

Listen to others

I'd had a problem with anger for many years and then the Lord took me through some healing and counselling. The teaching I received on anger during this time was exactly what I needed. It helped me to allow myself to feel angry but not wallow in it or allow it to become out of control. Instead, I felt the emotion and reached out to God – letting Him be responsible for the judgment of the person who had wronged me. I also realised how important it was for me to forgive the other person.

Jayne

For as long as I can remember I have been someone who becomes very anxious when faced with new situations. This would prevent me from doing many things and, however hard I tried, I didn't seem to be able to stop feeling anxious. When I was taught that behind anxiety can be an uncertain goal and that I can manage my emotions, it opened the door for a dramatic change in my life. I began to approach my anxiety by asking myself questions and talking to myself: 'What's uncertain about the situation I am facing? What's the worst that can happen? What strategies can I have up my sleeve if I am faced with the worst-case scenario?' Life is so much better!

Charlotte

Take it deeper

An important part of handling emotions well is to take responsibility for ourselves and our own emotions. No one else can make us feel a particular way; it is our own response, our perception of a situation and what we tell ourselves about it that results in feelings. Rather than saying to others: 'You made me feel … when … happened', we must own our emotions: 'When … happened, I felt …'.

Can you think of a situation when you didn't take responsibility and blamed someone else for how you felt?

Looking back on the event, with the knowledge you have gained from this session, how could you have dealt with this differently?

Think of some examples from your own life where you can trace:
- A *blocked goal* behind your anger
- An *unreachable goal* behind your guilt
- An *uncertain goal* behind your anxiety

Prayer

Lord, even though I sometimes wish that I didn't have certain emotions (and, at times, I can feel overwhelmed by them) I want to thank You that You made me with the capacity to feel. Having the capacity to feel negative emotions means that I also have the capacity to feel joy and happiness. Amen.

SUGGESTED PRAYER THEMES

- To respond to emotions in a godly way and repent of the times that our responses have been destructive towards ourselves or others.
- To take responsibility for our own feelings, to ask God for forgiveness and to forgive ourselves for the times we have not done so.
- To be aware of other people's feelings and let them take responsibility for themselves.

Creative ideas

Tools needed:

1. Two people who are willing to role play a conversation demonstrating blocked goals
2. Two sheets of paper on which is written an outline of the conversation (however the role play works best when those involved 'ad lib')
3. These two people then take part in a telephone conversation, using the rough guide to help them

Cont'd

(We suggest that you make up your own scenario or base the role play on the following rough guide. Bear in mind that the use of typical words that illustrate demandingness, awfulising and self-devaluation (listed on p.60) will exacerbate any feelings experienced.)

Person A is unable to drive, following an operation, and is desperate to get to the shops and to church on Sunday. **Person B** has offered to assist, but in practice constantly lets down **Person A**, blocking his/her goal.

Just before the start of the 'Ask Yourself' section, the 'willing couple' carry out their role play.

Person A: 'Hi … thanks ever so much for offering to pick me up on Wednesday so I can get to the shops; I so need to get there …'
Person B: 'Actually, that's why I'm calling … I can't make Wednesday – my friend is popping over.'
Person A: 'Oh, OK, no worries, you said Thursday and Friday were possibilities … I can manage till Thursday. Did you say morning or afternoon was possible, I can't remember?'
Person B: 'Err … afternoon. Oh, I've just remembered, I've already got something on Thursday afternoon'.
Person A: 'Friday?'
Person B: 'Yep, Friday's fine … I'll come for you at 10.00 am and we'll have several hours then, and I'll pick you up for church too, if you like.'
Person A: 'Oh, thanks, I'm really getting cabin fever not getting out of the house.'

Cont'd

End of call ... a few minutes later the phone rings and **Person A** answers.

Person B: 'I forgot ... I've got such a busy day on Friday, I can't fit a trip to the shops in.'
Person A: 'Oh ... but you can still do church on Sunday?'
Person B: 'This Sunday ... No! I've got a car full'.
Continue ad libbing ...

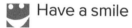 ## Have a smile

Dear God,

Maybe Cain and Abel would not have killed each other if they had been given their own rooms. It works with me and my brother.

Larry

Dear God,

I bet it is very hard for You to love all of everybody in the whole world. There are only four people in our family and I can never do it.

Nan**

---

1   For a comprehensive list of different emotions see *Beyond Chaotic Eating*, Helena Wilkinson (Surrey: RoperPenberthy Publishing, 2001) – visit: www.helenawilkinson.co.uk

**   See copyright page.

Safeguarding our bodies

An illness of the mind is an illness of the body, and vice versa.

(Madrianne Arvore)

As we conclude the workbook with this final session, let us reconsider how, in the beginning, Adam and Eve were created by God in His image as emotional, choosing, thinking and longing beings (in a physical form) and how, prior to the Fall, they had perfection in all of these areas. Their decision to act independently from God brought brokenness. We, too, now live with less than the ideal in every area of our lives. We can't ignore the fact that all aspects of the self are intertwined and when these are functioning well together they make for health and peak performance. However, when one area is not functioning well, it has a knock-on effect on the others. This includes the physical.

Safeguarding our bodies is taking care of them and endeavouring to make the most of them. This doesn't mean attaining physical perfection (were such a thing possible), and neither does it mean becoming obsessed with the body in any way. It simply means respecting ourselves as God's creation and recognising that our bodies are the temple of the Holy Spirit (1 Cor. 6:19). It is necessary to understand how we, as women, function physically, hence helping us to make the most of ourselves; it also means understanding how physical struggles affect us emotionally, and visa versa.

Looking at the creation of woman we see that God intended

us to be different from man. After He created Adam, 'The LORD God said, "It is not good for the man to be alone. I will make a helper suitable for him"' (Gen. 2:18). Out of the man God created Eve; made in the image of God and God's first model of womanhood. She was uniquely created, not as a second man or simply to be a helper to Adam, but as a *woman*, to fulfil a purpose that man could not.

Naked and unashamed, beautiful inside (because there was nothing marred about her), she related first to God and then to Adam and she had perfect physical functioning. How some of us wish we had perfect physical functioning! Although Eve had perfection in her body, she lost it; through the Fall her physical functioning changed dramatically. The ageing process and physical decline of the body came into being, along with many physical effects throughout life. Eve was told that she would experience pain in childbirth, and we have suffered ever since with physical and hormonal struggles such as: premenstrual symptoms, menopause, hormone imbalances etc.

The hormonal changes and imbalances in our body can affect our emotional, and even our spiritual, wellbeing. One of the key elements in worsening hormonal imbalances is stress (which is a clear example of how our physical and emotional functioning interrelate). We currently exist in an age where many live with constant stress. Instead of occasional, intense demands in our lives followed by rest, we have the tendency to be over-worked, involved in complex forms of relating with a variety of people, inadequately nourished due to adulterated food and we are also exposed to numerous environmental toxins.

Stress arises as a result of pressure and overload in the area of our mind and emotions; its negative consequences on the body are numerous. Some of the effects are: sleeplessness, lack of concentration, headaches, appetite and weight changes, lack of energy, stomach and bowel problems, change in blood pressure, physical aches and pains, poor immune functioning.

According to helpful information seen recently on a women's website, when our minds and bodies are challenged in any way it creates a demand on the adrenal glands. We all know the endless kind of challenges we face as women in today's world: lack of sleep, the threat of job loss, a demanding boss, personality conflicts, dieting, financial pressures, relationship problems, conflicts of personality, concern over teenagers, responsibility to elderly parents, death or illness of loved ones, conflicting roles at home, work and church, unresolved emotional issues, illness or infection, digestive disorders, poor eating habits, reliance on stimulants like caffeine and sugary foods, under- or over-exercise, to name but a few.

As a result our adrenal glands are continually on high alert ... and cortisol helps us to meet these challenges we face by converting proteins into energy, releasing glycogen and counteracting inflammation. This may be sustainable in the short term. But if these high levels continue over a longer period, the cortisol gradually erodes the body. Sustained high cortisol levels destroy healthy muscle and bone, slow down healing and delay normal cell regeneration. Adrenal fatigue may be a factor in many related conditions, including fibromyalgia, hypothyroidism, chronic fatigue syndrome, arthritis and premature menopause, amongst others.

There are a number of things you can do to care for your body and to help prevent stress, so that you honour God with your *whole* being: body, mind and spirit.

- **Thank God**. Spend time praising and thanking God. Praise has a positive effect on us. Thank Him for the body you have and ask Him to help you take care of it.

- **Consider the temple**. In recognising that our bodies are 'the temple of the Holy Spirit' we need to choose to take care of the temple in the best way we can.

- **Seek medical help**. When our bodies are sick we can seek help to restore as much as is possible in the circumstances.

- **Examine your self-talk**. Are irrational thoughts and wrong goals increasing your stress levels?

- **Seek emotional help**. If there are past hurts, issues on your mind or life patterns that cause problems to you or others, seek help to resolve these (this may involve professional help, prayer or talking with a friend).

- **Build healthy friendships**. Try to avoid friendships which are destructive and concentrate on those where there is mutual respect. Find someone with whom you can build an open and honest relationship, whereby you process what is on your mind and how you are feeling on a regular basis.

- **Ensure you have rest**. Our bodies are designed to rest and sleep in order to restore themselves and we can ensure that they receive adequate amounts of rest.

- **Take time to relax**. Given that stress causes breakdown in our bodies, we can build in times of relaxation: listening to music, reading a book, meditating on God's Word, enjoying God's creation, painting and so on.

- **Keep active**. Our bodies are designed to be exercised; to be kept flexible we need to find the most suitable form of exercise for us as individuals.

- **Eat healthily**. Nutrition plays an important part in the functioning of our bodies and affects us both physically and emotionally. Try to follow a basic diet of plenty of fruit and vegetables, complex carbohydrates, limited sugar and caffeine, animal fat and dairy products but plenty of essential fatty acids (nuts, seeds, olive oil, sesame oil), fish and at least six glasses of water a day.

- **Ensure a balance**. Think ahead about how you're going to spend your time, and work to maintain a balance of work and play, giving and receiving. Endeavour to set limits on work and to pursue interests and hobbies.

- **Endeavour not to deal with stress in unhealthy ways**. This includes drinking too much alcohol, consuming too much caffeine, misusing prescription drugs, smoking, over- or undereating.

We must do the best we can to take care of our bodies without becoming obsessive about them. As a spiritual act of worship, we can offer our bodies as living sacrifices, holy and pleasing to God (Rom. 12:1), not hate them nor live in fear of them and their potentially wayward ways: '… our bodies were made … for the Lord, and the Lord cares about our bodies … Don't you realize that your bodies are actually parts of Christ? ... Don't you realize that your body is the temple of the Holy Spirit, who lives in you and was given to you by God? You do not belong to yourself ...' (1 Cor. 6:13,15,19, NLT).

 # Explore the Bible

Read 1 Corinthians 6:12–20

 # Ask yourself

- We have looked at the role that stress can play in affecting us physically and emotionally and hence spiritually too.

How would you describe your current stress levels?

What steps can you take to lessen stress in your life?

What change do you think this will make to your spiritual life?

. . . .

Listen to others

I'm an Associate Minister in a growing church, surrounded by people, and fairly self-sufficient – or so I thought. The only persistent failure in my life was being three stones overweight, and this baffled me because in every other area of my life I am very disciplined. However, even though I tried (and failed) over and over again to solve the problem, I did not believe there could be any emotional reason for this failure; indeed I saw myself as a whole person and refused to make the 'excuse' of eating to comfort myself in any way.

As part of a sabbatical, I chose to attend a women's course, which proved to be a real journey of self-discovery. I came to understand that although I am surrounded by people at work, I had, in fact, been feeling rather isolated; and on discovering that I am an extrovert personality, I saw that isolation drains my strength. I also realised that in all my quiet times I was constantly storing things up for the next sermon – and my prayers usually revolved around church business, and my family. However, I learned that I had been experiencing a lot of negative emotions, without ever questioning where they came from; fear and low self-esteem had become normal for me. On the course, we were taught to 'catch' our thoughts, to discover what we are saying to ourselves when we worry about things.

The outcome of these revelations was that I decided I needed the support and friendship of other women – and alongside some of the ladies in our church, we have now established a women's ministry. In addition I am meeting regularly with ladies in ministry in other churches and, together, we are putting on events for other female leaders in the central region.

Something someone said really grabbed my attention: 'embrace your femininity'. At the time I realised that I had no idea what that really meant, but I have come to realise it has to do with being comfortable as a woman in ministry, and set free from having to think or act like a man, in what is a very male-orientated profession.

And so I believe it was in an attempt to embrace my femininity that I allowed myself to consider just the possibility that there might be emotional reasons for my overeating, asking myself questions such as: 'Are there any irrational thoughts that cause me to fail?' 'Am I "rewarding" myself with food?'

I hardly know how it happened, but the result of these reflections was that I lost two and a half stone and dropped three dress sizes.

I'd like to say that was the end of my eating disorder, but I have discovered that I very easily slip back into bad habits, and even into the tendency to fix the problem by sheer willpower (which never works) instead of catching the thoughts that drive me into self-destructive behaviour. For this reason, I need to remind myself that God worked very powerfully in my life, and will do so again; and I need to come back to God, time and time again, asking Him to help me to put into practice what I learned at Waverley and to *take captive every thought to make it obedient to Christ'* (2 Cor. 10:5).

Rosemary

Take it deeper

- Women are renowned for not liking their bodies or at least wanting some change!

  Given that your body is the temple of the Holy Spirit, can you choose to view it differently from the way we are all encouraged to by the media (and not to constantly compare yourself with unattainable or unsustainable ideals)?

  Are there changes that it would be helpful to make to your eating and exercise patterns in order to take care of your body and keep it as healthy as you can?

Prayer

Lord, it is awesome that You have chosen, through Your Holy Spirit, to dwell within me. I ask that each day I would grasp a greater revelation of the significance of this. Open my eyes, I pray, to see the ways in which I damage Your temple and help me to honour You in all ways. Amen.

SUGGESTED PRAYER THEMES

- Repentance for not taking care of your body (and, for some people, even abusing it).
- For greater awareness of how the physical, emotional and spiritual are interconnected and affect each other.
- For healing for parts of your body which are not functioning as they should or are disabled; and for physical sickness.

Creative ideas

At the end of this final session ask the group, as a conclusion, to read the 'Quick spiritual checkup'.

 Have a smile

A little girl, born with a cleft palate, was embarrassed that she didn't look and talk like the rest of the children in her class. When asked about her lip, she would just say that it was the result of an accident.

One day, a school nurse, giving her a hearing test, whispered in her ear: 'I wish you were my little girl.' From that day she was changed.

God has been whispering the same thing in our ears since the days of Eden.*

---

* See copyright page.

Quick spiritual checkup

When you find yourself moving off course spiritually, carry out the following checkup:

1. Consider if there may be physical problems contributing to your difficulties, such as overwork, stress, lack of sleep, poor nutrition, allergies etc.
2. Challenge any thinking that is causing problems and work at replacing it with thoughts which are both rational and biblical.
3. Identify the dominant negative emotion. Remember there are three streams of problem emotions: anger and resentment; guilt and shame; anxiety and fear.
4. Ask yourself what the emotion is telling you about your goals. Anger suggests a blocked or undermined goal; anxiety an uncertain goal; guilt an unreachable goal.
5. Attempt to focus on the goal you might be pursuing which may be contributing to your problems.
6. Seek to analyse the wrong thinking that may be providing the energy for the pursuit of that goal (Example: *'I must have constant praise if I am to stay a secure person'*).
7. Re-establish proper goals. A simple formula to remember is that most problems arise because of the pursuit of wrong goals, based on wrong thinking about how to experience security, significance and self-worth. Remember the apostle Paul's wise advice: ' … we make it our goal to please him …' (2 Cor. 5:9). This is a goal that is certain, reachable and can never be undermined.

It's in Christ that we find out who we are
and what we are living for.
Long before we first heard of Christ
and got our hopes up,
he had his eye on us, had designs on us
for glorious living,
part of the overall purpose he is working out
in everything and everyone.

Taken from Ephesians 1 – The Message

Notes for group leaders

1. Ensure that everyone in the group has their own workbook.

2. Prepare the '**Creative Ideas**' in advance of the session.

3. Encourage people to look over any material they have missed prior to coming to the session.

4. Have at hand a list of people/organisations to whom you can make a referral if anyone in the group is struggling with a complex issue.

5. Consider purchasing in advance some of the recommended reading books for people to look at or buy.

6. Encourage people to go over the session again on their own to reinforce what they have learned.

7. Endeavour to 'draw out' the quieter people in the group to ensure even input into the session.

8. In the last session, include a time of feedback for people to reflect on the ways in which they have benefited from the workbook.

Recommended reading

Beyond Chaotic Eating, Helena Wilkinson (Horsham: RoperPenberthy Publishing, 2001)

Boundaries: When to Say Yes, How to Say No, To Take Control of Your Life, Dr. Henry Cloud & Dr. John Townsend (Grand Rapids: Zondervan, 2002)

Breaking Free from Loneliness, Helena Wilkinson (Horsham: RoperPenberthy Publishing, 2004)

Changes That Heal: How to Understand the Past to Ensure a Healthier Future, Dr. Henry Cloud (Grand Rapids: Zondervan, 1997)

Christ Empowered Living, Selwyn Hughes (Farnham: CWR, 2002)

Connecting: Healing Ourselves and Our Relationships, Larry Crabb (Nashville: Word Publishing, 2005)

Inspiring Women – Created as a Woman, Beverley Shepherd (Farnham: CWR, 2007)

Inspiring Women – Finding Freedom, Helena Wilkinson (Farnham: CWR, 2007)

Inspiring Women – True Confidence, Wendy Bray (Farnham: CWR, 2008)

Love Beyond Reason: Moving God's Love from Your Head to Your Heart, John Ortberg, (Grand Rapids: Zondervan, 2001)

Mirror Mirror: Discover Your True Identity in Christ, Graham Beynon (Nottingham: IVP, 2008)

Safe People: How to Find Relationships That Are Good for You and Avoid Those That Aren't, Dr. Henry Cloud & Dr. John Townsend (Grand Rapids: Zondervan, 1996)

Taming Your Emotional Tigers, Tony Ward (Leicester: IVP, 1998)

Telling Yourself the Truth, William Backus & Marie Chapian (Ada, MI: Bethany House, 2000)

The Secret Things of God: Unlocking the Treasures Reserved for You, Dr. Henry Cloud (London: Simon & Schuster Ltd, 2007)

Who Am I? Discovering Your Identity in Christ, Mary Pytches (London: Hodder & Stoughton, 1999)

Day and Residential Courses

Counselling Training

Leadership Development

Biblical Study Courses

Regional Seminars

Ministry to Women

Daily Devotionals

Books and Videos

Conference Centre

Trusted all Over the World

CWR HAS GAINED A WORLDWIDE reputation as a centre of excellence for Bible-based training and resources. From our headquarters at Waverley Abbey House, Farnham, England, we have been serving God's people for over 40 years with a vision to help apply God's Word to everyday life and relationships. The daily devotional *Every Day with Jesus* is read by nearly a million readers an issue in more than 150 countries, and our unique courses in biblical studies and pastoral care are respected all over the world. Waverley Abbey House provides a conference centre in a tranquil setting.

For free brochures on our seminars and courses, conference facilities, or a catalogue of CWR resources, please contact us at the following address:

CWR, Waverley Abbey House, Waverley Lane, Farnham, Surrey GU9 8EP, UK

Telephone: +44 (0)1252 784700
Email: mail@cwr.org.uk
Website: www.cwr.org.uk

CWR Applying God's Word *to everyday life and relationships*

How to be a Secure Woman

by Jeannette Barwick and Catherine Butcher

Where can women find security in this insecure world? Using examples of women in the Bible and women today, you will learn practical steps that will lead to the lasting security found only in a relationship with God.

Eight sessions for individual or group use.

96-page paperback, 148x210mm
ISBN: 978-1-85345-307-6
£5.99

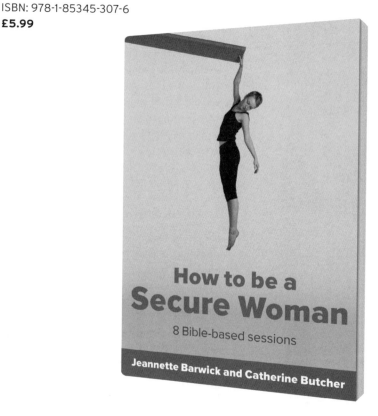

How to be a Secure Woman 40-day Devotional

by Catherine Butcher

Identify where you go for security and why you don't find lasting satisfaction – and discover how to obtain true and enduring security from God.

This devotional condenses key points from the life-changing How to be a Secure Woman seminar into short daily readings.

112-page paperback, 106x165mm
ISBN: 978-1-85345-391-5
£4.99

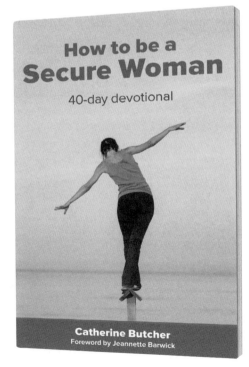

Inspiring Women Every Day

by various women authors

Daily Bible-reading notes written by women, for women, to inspire and encourage all ages:

- Increase your faith and ignite your passion for Jesus
- Find practical support to face life's challenges
- Be enlightened by insights into God's Word.

64-page booklet, 120x170mm, published bimonthly
ISSN: 1478-050X
£13.80 UK annual subscription (six issues)
Individual copies: **£2.49 each**